Chino SL Designs

Published by Chino SL Designs (USA) First Printing June 2016

© Copyright 2016 by CHINO SL Designs. All rights preserved. Except as permitted under the United States Copyright Act of 1976, no part of this publication may be produced or distributed in any form or by any means, or stored in a database or retrieval system, without the prior written permission of CHINO SL Designs.

Please do not participate in or encourage piracy of copyrighted materials in violation of author's rights. Purchase only authorized editions.

Caution: All rights whatsoever in this play – including stock and amateur rights in the USA – are strictly reserved and application for performance, etc., should be made before rehearsal to Stacy Lamar King at stacylamarking@gmail.comRegistered Trademark

Library of Commerce Cataloging-In-Publication-Data King, Stacy
Where There's Faith There's Grace: A play in three acts

Printed in the United States of America
ISBN: 9780692739181
Library of Congress Control Number:

This is a work of fiction. Names, characters, places, and incidents either are the product of the author's imagination or are used fictitiously, and any resemblance to actual persons, living or dead, businesses, companies, events, or locales is purely incidental.

For Jesus Christ, the

Son of God

Who came to Earth

And Lived and Died as the Son of Man

So that we might live forever with God

In Heaven

Introduction

A man and a woman had a little baby and there were three in that family. Only Stacy could make that work. Many of us know the story of marriage and family because most of us have lived it. But do we truly know this story, the love story of God, Jesus, Joseph, and Mary?

God has always used ordinary people to do extraordinary things. Only in this world, as it is right now, could we believe that God had somehow removed himself from exercising this fundamental part of himself. Only in this world, could we lose faith in God's provision to do the extraordinary things with each one of us.

God shared an idea with Stacy some 20 years ago, an idea that he shared with only one other person at the time, and that person was me. I don't know why, I've never asked why, and Stacy has never told me why. That's just Stacy. An open and closed book to those he gives the key.

Stacy has done so much in his life, yet is as humble as they come. He assists anyone in need, inspires the uninspired, and is not afraid to tell his story of poverty and abuse. He is a man who was mercifully stripped of the trappings of this world so that he could see the one mission, his only mission, which was to do his part and to help those who are lost yet want to be found.

I met Stacy in Quantico, Virginia in 1991. Somehow life's events had brought him to work in the Marine Corps Exchange at Marine Corps Base, Quantico. Abandoned in 1991 by family, he slowly allowed us to become his adopted family and we watched a broken man crawl, walk, and then run back to being true to himself, learn to love himself, and learn to start over.

Little did I know that this man would have to use these very skills once again in 2015 while dealing with the same act by the same people. He's no quitter and he's no whiner. He's a proud black man, who through God possesses this amazing ability to survive over and over again in life.

Stacy would later confess that what I really saw was God's ability to give us all the endurance to stay under the test until we have learned what he wanted us to learn from it. Explaining it in true Stacy fashion, he echoed that, "the same God," who knows us all, knows those that would do us harm just as well."

Stacy believes that God gives the inflictor and the injured the same warning to protect themselves from themselves. And that we find ourselves in discomfort when we fail to heed God's ample and detailed warnings. I love this man's mind.

Stacy never took work more serious than he did the relationships he had formed with those caught up in the same grind that consumes us all, which is making more junk that people really don't need so that we can get paid to buy more junk that we really don't need. In his mind, we should be drug tested and often.

Stacy made everyone laugh at the ridiculousness of life as man wants to live it. He says he laughs because God created laughter to show us just that ridiculousness. How else could God deal with his always wayward children? It has been truly amazing how God allowed us to get so close and to maintain this friendship for 25 years! We can talk about anything and argue about everything when he's open to talking!

To love him, you must understand that part of this man. In order to not be hurt or disappointed by his frequent and unanticipated disappearances from the world. What he taught me is that our inner beauty (God's divine impact) is the greatest gift we can share with one another. With that degree of sharing, we shouldn't add additional requirements to one another. Stacy is truly my brother in Christ!

Now, about this play, "Where There's Faith, There's Grace," let's just say I was not prepared for the final product. This is truly one of the best love stories I have ever read! It touches every human and spiritual emotion and has practical lessons for every real relationship in my life.

I have never looked at the birth of Jesus through the lens of two kids who had been entrusted with the greatest responsibility God has ever bestowed on a man and woman before or since. It is the story of unconditional love, unyielding faith, total belief, iron clad trust, strength of character, mutual respect, and empathy. There isn't a single husband or wife who can't benefit from the words within this manuscript.

When I finished reading it, I wanted to call Stacy immediately because it moved me to tears. I know it will have the same impact on others. I know it can and will move many of our young people back to the source of everything beautiful, the only God who proudly proclaimed to the Universe that "I Am He."

God's love can be seen in all that it touches and I can see how he has used this ordinary man from meager means to do extraordinary things so that God's light might be made to manifest through him. After all, we are all simply stories caught within other stories, trying to find our place to sit, read, be read, and become Love.

My hope for this beautiful piece of work, is that it will cause everyone who sees the play or reads the manuscript, to begin to allow the love of God to over-take them so that they might find God and live forever with him in Heaven.

1 Peter 4:8 New King James Version (NKJV)

And above all things have fervent love for one another, for "love will cover a multitude of sins."

- Lisa A. Cobb

Dedication

To everyone I have met along my path.

Each of you in your own unique way has left a mark on my soul that will endure forever

Where There's Faith

There's Grace

A Play in 3 Acts

By Stacy Lamar King

© 2016 by Stacy Lamar King

DBA Chino SL Designs

28425 N Black Canyon Hwy

Phoenix AZ 85085

stacylamarking@gmail.com

Table of Contents

Characters ii

Setting iii

The Play iv

Act One - Scene One - Love 1

Act One - Scene 2 - A Woman's Worth 11

Act One - Scene Three - With This Ring 25

Act Two - Scene One - The Fork in the Road 29

Act Two - Scene Two - When Doves Try 37

Act Two - Scene Three - The Reasons Why 47

Act Three - Scene One - I Do 51

CHARACTERS

JOSEPH DAVIDSON	The Painter Who Works With His Hands
MARY GRACE	The Fiancée' of Joseph
GABE	The Messenger of the Lord
ANGEL	The Angel of the Lord
DJ SOUL	The Voice of the City
AMAZING GRACE	The Mother of Mary
JOE SR.	The Father of Joseph
LIZ BETH	The Mother of Jon
ZACH	The Father of Jon
MINISTER	The Messenger of the Congregation

The Setting

It is a non-descript non-descript one-room, studio apartment in North Charleston, South Carolina. It is everything that Mary has dreamed of and nothing that she hasn't. Mary has the low rent she required to match her skinny but adequate income.

Mary is living happily in her Top Ramen world, which is reminiscent of her favorite Robert De Niro line from Heat, "Never get attached to anything you are not willing to walk out on in 30 seconds if the heat is on."

Mary's checklist at move-in; Futon - check, folding table - check, bean bag chair – check, cell phone - check, laptop - check, internet - check, natural hair – you know it, Taser from Dad – double-check, nun-chucks from little brother – the opposite of check, and the word from her mother – check – check, thank you Lord.

The apartment complex was neat, clean, quiet, and teeming with other freshmen like her who were away from home tackling the world, scared to death, but too proud to say so.

A painting of Ruby Dee is her prized possession from her mother, and it hangs as the sole piece of art in a room of sterility and neutral paint.

It is late morning and Charleston is alive with the sounds of its people.

The Play

After the Light was Gone

The voice of God has not been heard in this world for centuries. It appears to many that God has been a silent witness to it all, as if he withdrew from this world while it became its ripest with the fruits of its evil toils.

Silence, in response to this question, is never truly silent. The absence of the beauty found within the word, is the result of the horrible decisions, made by spirits and humans, which resulted from the inappropriate use of God's gift of free will.

The love of the lie has reinforced the ancient evil that never rests, who prowls the world like a hungry lion, yet most often appears in the form of a wolf wearing sheep's clothing.

Screams are screamed, yet never heard, by a world too busy satisfying its desire for carnal trappings. And the Church said nothing, and did nothing, because it, itself, had become the wolf that paraded itself in the lamb's wool. It had become the ancient evil.

Faith had been fractured by man's desire for power, leaving the flock uncovered; forced to choose between the forces that use tradition to impose their will, the forces that use the Word to effect their wars, the forces that isolate their followers from the world and God, and the forces that believe that their superiority was ordained by God.

You could cut the tension in this world with a sword.

As a result, the faithful became exiles within their own communities and countries. A new reality burst forward, where fear led to more fear, and more fear led to distrust, and distrust to intolerance. The condition known as Spiritual Darkness.

Where There's Faith There's Grace

Alas, there is hope in the certainty that is found in the Word. The Word is a force so strong that there is nothing that the lie can do to remove it. And wouldn't that be the truest indication that God is not who he says he is, and that the ancient evil was really what he claimed to be?

And, isn't that the only possible outcome when two opposing Kings fight for possession of a common prize? That one might perish for all to see, never to be seen or spoken of again? I ask you which of these "two" Kings has made such a statement and which has not? The answer to this question tells you what you already know to be true.

The time of the Lamb is upon us, and a young obscure couple, strong in faith, limited by positon, who are strengthened and reinforced by their belief in the light, the all-powerful God, will demonstrate a love so deep that it is the example that all couples can emulate and follow.

Life was dread, dead, and dying, and in the blink of an eye it happened, a Miracle, because,

A man and a woman had a little baby
Yeah they did
And there were three in the family
That's my favorite number
I said three
That's my favorite number

Stacy Lamar King

Where There's Faith There's Grace

Act One
Scene One
Love

It is the winter of 2015. Mary sits in her one room studio apartment, gazing at pictures of wedding rings and bridal dresses, all the while singing songs of love about her favorite guy in the whole wide world, Mr. Joseph Davidson.

Mary is very much the quintessential teen, full of life, an eternal optimist, and a beautiful petite young lady whose faith allows her to see beyond her sins. It is this uniqueness that fuels the smile that everyone who knows her never ends. This smile has illuminated every decision, big or small, that she has made and will make in the future.

It is Friday afternoon, also known as, "TGIF" time. How appropriate. Mary's mother, Amazing, who happens to have the most AMAZING name ever, was coming over later after work to have a little "girl" talk.

These were the adult conversations that preceded the "Mommy" and "Me" talks that had recently passed because they were no longer the context in which these two women needed to speak.

Amazing is on her way. She is leaving the hospital after her 12-hour shift concludes and taking the long roads through town in order to avoid the freeway. The hospital was her home away from home. It was the place where Mary's father, Clyde, affectionately called, "the place the living go to die." A comment that after all of these years is still met with Amazing's stink eye.

Momma's talks have always been special to Mary. This talk wouldn't be any different. So Mary floats through the air, singing throughout the apartment, and listening to DJ Soul who has been her favorite radio personality since forever.

Noting that when a woman sings in her home, you'd best believe she's happy.

DJ Soul:	"Good morning Chuck-Town. This next one is going out to Mary from Amazing."
DJ Soul:	"That's right a real throw-back. Here's "The Way" by Jill Scott."
DJ Soul:	"Mary your momma said, "sing it like you wrote it Baby Girl."

(Mary fills the tiny apartment with song and dance. She takes a seat after her song ends with thoughts of Joseph the Painter on her mind. Suddenly, there is a knock at the door.)

Mary:	"Momma I know that's you? I would know that knock anywhere."

(Mary rushes to open the door to greet her mother. Mary and Amazing gracefully embrace pulling back slowly to look at one another like it was the first time they had ever met.)

Amazing:	"Oh look at my precious little baby. Girl we miss you like crazy."
Mary:	"Momma you do know I've only been gone three days."
Amazing:	"Girl tell that to your father."

(Amazing and her daughter shake their heads and laugh quietly.)

Amazing:	"Mary I could hear you singing clear across the street. Girl, you know a woman's happy when she's singing throughout her home."
Amazing:	"It's Joseph, isn't it?"
Mary:	"Uh huh." (Mary smiles sheepishly.)
Amazing:	"Let me guess he's on your mind all of the time."

(Mary ponders this with her hand to her chin knowing that no answer is needed. It's a rhetorical question for sure.)

Amazing:	"I bet you can't sleep even when you're too tired to stand. Am I right?"

Mary:	"Momma, now you know I can sleep through anything."
Amazing:	"Oh, that may be true but I know every word he says sounds like a big ole bag of penny candy."
Amazing:	"You just can't get enough of them, hmmmm?"

(Mary nods sheepishly.)

Mary:	"Momma, now what's this penny candy you speak of?"
Amazing:	"Baby it's old school."
Amazing:	"You gotta do that research for yourself. But when you figure it out please let me know, because you got it bad girl."
Mary:	"Momma, I get it from you and Daddy."
Mary:	"How can I ever forget the way Daddy sings to you? Especially when he plays the same Marvin Gaye song over and over again every year on your anniversary."
Mary:	"And when he puts that dance with it, oh myyyyyy, it's to die for."
Mary:	"My girlfriends and I still talk about it to this very day."
Amazing:	"Mary I can tell you this much. It never gets old to me."
Amazing:	"Every time I hear it, I remember all the years we've shared together. My life literally flashes before my eyes."
Amazing:	"Through the thick and thin, it's the little things that define our life together."
Amazing:	"When I hear it, I hear our story, in his words, in his song."

Mary:	"Momma you have to write this down one day. It's poetic. It's magical."
Amazing:	"I'm writing it on your heart right now. Now Mary, on a serious note."
Amazing:	"I wouldn't be your momma, if I didn't' share with you the simple and yet most profound words that my mother shared with me when I was about your age rushing head-on into adulthood."
Amazing:	"She told me that these words had been handed down from mother to daughter since, well, Eve."
Mary:	"Momma do you know who actually started this family tradition?"
Amazing:	"Mary, truth be told I don't think anyone, who is still alive, really knows who started it all."
Amazing:	"So I choose to believe that it has been a part of this family always."
Mary:	"I love the way you talk Momma."
Amazing:	"Thank you Baby."
Amazing:	"My Momma started the conversation just like this."

(Amazing takes a seat on the couch and Mary follows and sits on the floor right next to her, just like she has done since the days of "Mommy and Me" time.)

Amazing:	"She said, "Earthly love can hurt sometimes, but Heavenly love heals and uplifts you every time.""
Mary:	"What did she mean Momma?"
Amazing:	"It's like this baby, love is complicated."
Amazing:	"It means you're going to go through some things, some hard things, the kind of things that can tear the two of you apart."
Amazing:	"Especially if you forget about or stop believing in the Lord's power to heal the hurt."

Mary:	"Momma, are you saying that these feelings that I have for Joseph are going to change when Joseph and I get older?"
Amazing:	"Not at all baby." **(While nodding her head yes.)**

(Mary is puzzled by the mixed message.)

Amazing:	"What I am saying love, is that this life can cave in on you if you let it, and when that happens, you can easily forget about the intensity of these feelings of love."
Mary:	"So it's our perception that changes?"
Amazing:	"Yes Baby, it was just the window that you saw the world through at that moment."
Amazing:	"But when that happens, you have to continue to talk to the Lord, because He will lead you both back to the love you misplaced."
Amazing:	"Because He is love baby, and a big part of loving is learning the healing power that is found in forgivenes
Mary:	"So learning to love like the Lord is the key to it all?"
Amazing:	"Yes my Mini-Me."
Mary:	"Ha, Ma!! Mini-Me. Momma you sure can crack me up."
Amazing:	"Not trying to, trust me…. Just being your Momma."
Amazing:	"Joseph is a God-fearing man, with good values and morals, and your father and I love him just like we love you."
Amazing:	"I need you to remember that he got this far in life without you. So, don't make it your job to try to change him."
Amazing:	"It is, however, your responsibility to continuously remind him why you were drawn to him."

Amazing:	"To reassure him of his position as the head of your family. To let him know why you are so thankful that he exhibits the strengths of a man filled with the Word."
Mary:	"I see now Mom."
Mary:	"The arguments that my girlfriends tell me they've had with their boyfriends seem pretty darn petty after hearing your words."
Amazing:	"Baby, I am so glad you mentioned your girlfriends. And you can also tack on any male friends you have for that matter in order to for me to make my next point."
Amazing:	"You must never violate the trust within your relationship, your marriage, or your home."
Mary:	"Violate trust?"
Amazing:	"Yes baby, trust."
Amazing:	"Which means, keep what's yours, Joseph's, and your family, inside you, Joseph, and the home you share with them."
Mary:	"Like Vegas?"
Amazing:	"No, I'm not talking about secrets. I'm talking about establishing a place where everyone feels safe to share themselves."
Amazing:	"A place where they feel that their trust won't be violated to outsiders."
Amazing:	"Now will our actions at times require the involvement of outsiders? Most definitely. But that isn't what I'm talking about here."
Amazing:	"Do you understand?"
Mary:	"Yes I do. Thank you for clarifying."

Amazing:	"Where was I? Oh, this rule also applies to dealing with the families outside your home including your father and I."
Amazing:	"That is, unless it is something that must be reported or is something that the two of you lack the experience or knowledge to address without help."
Amazing:	"I will promise you this much. Your father and I, will never talk to either of you alone when you have an issue."
Amazing:	"Because that creates separation and that can negatively impact our relationship with one or possibly both of you."
Amazing:	"And quite possibly the relationship between your father and I."
Mary:	"Thanks for being real Momma."
Mary:	"I've always felt very awkward whenever someone told me something negative about a person that we both knew."
Mary:	"I'll definitely try much harder to shut these kinds of conversations down before they get started in the future."
Mary:	"Because ugly thoughts affect us all U-G-A-L-E-E, and who needs more of that?"
Amazing:	"Another very important point Mary is this."
Amazing:	"As hard as this may be to believe. Joseph will never be everything you need, so you need to remain cognizant of that."
Amazing:	"Because that is an impossible standard to try to meet and an awful expectation to try to satisfy."
Amazing:	"The same applies to you regarding Joseph's needs."

(Stop the presses.)

Mary:	"What could Joseph possibly need outside of me, Momma?"
Amazing:	"Mary close your eyes please, now open them, do you see any stars floating around that head of yours?"
Mary:	"Noooo."
Mary:	"Ohhhhh, I get it."
Mary:	"I'm not the center of the universe, and as hard as it may be, for me to believe, Joseph will always have other interests outside of me."
Amazing:	"Thank you."
Amazing:	"What I want more than anything for you two, is for you to be both real and realistic with one another from the beginning until the end."
Amazing:	"Because if forever is not the destination of this love you share, do not insult God's marital arrangement by doing it just for right now."
Mary:	"I'm feeling much more grounded now Momma, thank you for speaking life into me."
Amazing:	"You don't have to thank me, it's part of my job."
Amazing:	"Now on the cool side of the pillow, you two can always tell each other what you need from one another."
Amazing:	"But when you do, do that, ensure that your needs are aligned with the Word."
Amazing:	"You have to stay in the Word daily baby, because it's your protection."
Amazing:	"Last words about your home."
Amazing:	"It is the place where you and your family find peace from this wicked, wicked, world."
Amazing:	"Protect your home and your home will protect you."

Where There's Faith There's Grace

Amazing: "I almost forgot, there's one other thing."

Amazing: "You have to be predictable because men thrive off of it, and truth be told, they need it to breathe. Literally."

Mary: "Like oxygen?"

Amazing: "Just like oxygen."

Amazing: "Joseph needs your word to be your word, your intentions to be honorable, and your eyes to always be on the prize."

Mary: "What's the prize Momma?"

Amazing: "Helping one another gain the key to eternal life with God through His Word."

Mary: "Momma, this has been an amazing conversation. Thanks so much for coming clear across town after work to share your time and these wise words with me."

Mary: "I promise you and Daddy, that even when my head is in the clouds, my feet, because of the way you've raised me, and keep teaching me, will always remain firmly perched on solid ground."

Amazing: "Thank you baby. I needed to hear that. You're our one and only daughter and in the big scheme of things we know our remaining time with you is measured."

Amazing: "You're going to spend most of your life on this Earth without us, but our words will keep us alive in you always.

Amazing: "You can always find us in the words we've shared with you."

Amazing: "But when you do lose your way, and you will, always trust in the Lord and he will show you the way back."

(Mary's smile beams across her face and off the eyes of Amazing.)

Amazing: "Now baby, I have got to get on home now. Your father is about to get up soon to get ready for the night shift."

Amazing: "He'll need my help finding something and I'll be there to help because the help is more important to him than the thing he's looking for."

Amazing: "It is a dance we've danced all of our lives together, it's just that thing we do."

Mary smiles because she understood in this moment the meaning Behind the "dance" she has witnessed between her parents for many years. Amazing and Mary stood together to bring an end to their girl talk. They walked slowly towards the door exchanging small talk, cute smiles, and words of encouragement. As they reached the door, they hugged and then pulled back to look intimately into each other's eyes as if it were the last time they'd see each other. Leaving nothing unsaid.

Mary: "I love you forever Momma."

Amazing: "I love you forever too Baby."

Mary looked out the door until her mother was safely in her car. And once she was in the car, Amazing waited patiently for Mary to close the door and flash her living room light, signaling that she was safe and secure for the night.

(Curtains.)

Act One

Scene 2

A Woman's Worth

The sun sneaks up on Joseph and Joe Sr. who are sitting in the rear of the paint shop drinking their favorite cup of joe, while eating the usual, the same PB&J sandwich they have shared since Joseph's early apprenticeship days. Today's conversation will be unlike any they have had before. Joe Sr. is going to share his story and his song and Joseph is going to learn a woman's worth.

Joe Sr.:	"Joseph, I can see why you love this girl the way you do."
Joe Sr.:	"She's sharp as a tack and nothing like these young girls out here."
Joseph:	"It's like they say Dad, "There's something about Mary.""

(Joseph winks at his father.)

Joseph:	"She is special and I know she's going to leave her mark on this world."
Joseph:	"I'm so sure of it, but for the life of me, I don't know what she's going to do."
Joe Sr.:	"You don't need to know everything Joseph. That wouldn't make life worth living."
Joe Sr.:	"Now would it?"
Joseph:	"No Sir. I guess not."
Joe Sr.:	"You're a Davidson and that wouldn't suit you at all."
Joseph:	"Dad you know me too well."

(Joe Sr. nods and shrugs his shoulders like "who knew.")

Joe Sr.:	"Joseph, the best advice I can give you is this, scoop that young lady up and hang on to her forever."
Joe Sr.:	"Because a blind man could see that the two of you have something special to share with this world."
Joseph:	"Wow, really?"
Joe Sr.:	"Yes son, it ain't hard to tell."
Joe Sr.:	"Now, with that being said, let me bring you back from outer space."
Joe Sr.:	"You know that place young men go to when they are bitten by the love bug."
Joe Sr.:	"Now, women they can thrive up there, but men, let's just say we're not built to hang out there like we're on vacation."
Joe Sr.:	"That's why we need so many amenities up there. You know, special suits, masks, peanut butter & jelly, Sports Center, things like that."
Joseph:	"OK Dad, so why do the women go into space in the same rockets, wearing the same suits as the men?"
Joe Sr.:	"Really son?"
Joe Sr.:	"Firstly, they have to wear the suits because men still aren't ready for their level of awesomeness."
Joe Sr.:	"Secondly and most importantly, they can't send a bunch of men high on testosterone up there alone without adult supervision."
Joe Sr.:	"So, someone has to keep them from killing themselves up there."

(The father and son shake their heads and laugh.)

Joe Sr.:	"Now Joseph, please try to keep the questions to a minimum."
Joe Sr.:	"I need to get home before your mother starts calling every hospital in town."

Joseph:	"Gottttt it, don't ask questions that lead to more questions about questions."
Joe Sr.:	"Ha!"
Joe Sr.:	"Joseph, here's the skinny on women."
Joe Sr.:	"Even on Earth, where we (men), think we have some level of control, wrong, we don't."
Joe Sr.:	"So two things, once you put that ring on Mary's finger."
Joe Sr.:	"(1) the amount of time you have to talk goes from slim to almost none, (2) your woman is going to talk enough for the two of you."
Joe Sr.:	"Like the shark needs to move to stay alive, so does the woman with her talking."
Joseph:	"That's pretty extreme Dad."
Joe Sr.:	"Not meant to be. The world is going to beat you down a lot. It can make you not want to communicate."
Joe Sr.:	"She's going to have to speak for both of you during those moments you don't feel like talking to anyone."
Joe Sr.:	"Over time, you will learn to pick your times and your words very carefully."
Joe Sr.:	"There will be times you're going to be right there ready to answer a question, and she's going to cut in and answer it for you. Do not overreact."

(Joseph had a question but remained quiet.)

Joe Sr.:	"Especially when the one asking the question just happens to be of the female persuasion."
Joe Sr.:	"Roll with it son, because a real woman can sense the true intentions of another woman."

Joseph:	"Got it Dad, listen more, talk less, make all the decisions a husband is supposed to make, and leave the rest to Momma."
Joe Sr.:	"You're very close. But remember, even when you get to make decisions, you must make your ideas her ideas."
Joe Sr.:	"That's called buy-in in the business world. I think that's what they called it"
Joe Sr.:	"I call it good ole WIIFM, "What's in It for Me."
Joe Sr.:	"When your woman has a stake in the game she's more likely to help you write the plan."
Joe Sr.:	"And it's much harder for anyone to bash a decision they played a part in making."
Joseph:	"Wow Dad! That point there can be applied in almost every phase of my life."
Joseph:	"Where did you pick that up?"
Joe Sr.:	"Your Momma."

(Joseph howls with laughter.)

Joe Sr.:	"Great! Now that you understand those key points, we can move into part two of this conversation."
Joe Sr.:	"I call it finding your song."
Joseph:	"OK Dad. You totally lost me here. We've been to space and back and now we're writing songs?"
Joseph:	"Please show me how this has any bearing on my dealings with Mary."

(Joseph stands in quiet disbelief. Two questions and no reaction from his father.)

Joe Sr.:	"Glad you asked Junior. It's part of the Davidson story and it begins like this, "Once upon a time........"

Joseph:	"Oh my goodness, please tell me you're not going to tell me a fairytale."
Joe Sr.:	"Joseph every Davidson man has a story, not a tale about his song. Now get it right."

(Joseph couldn't prevent himself from rolling his eyes towards the Heavens.)

Joe Sr.:	"You're going to have to find your song so that you can write your own Davidson love story."
Joe Sr.:	"For starters make sure it's something easy to remember, and classy, because as difficult as it may seem, you're going to get OLD, QUICK!"
Joe Sr.:	"So make sure your song is something you'll be proud to sing in front of your great-grandchildren."
Joe Sr.:	"So that RAP mess is absolutely out of the question, just ball it up, throw it in the trash, and don't ever try to pull it back out!!!"
Joe Sr.:	"Do I even need to explain why?"
Joseph:	"No Dad. Rap is a bunch of bad words, naked women, and pool parties, where grown men with pet tigers, wearing jeans and timberland boots, mumble things that are wrapped up in the stolen music of real legends."
Joseph:	"Whewwwww. I still remember that."
Joe Sr.:	"Good, you were listening all these years. Make sure your kids get the message too. That stuff is poison for the soul."

(Joseph looks at his watch.)

Joe Sr.:	"Slow your roll Junior. You don't need to time me. I got this."
Joe Sr.:	"You only get one time, and I mean just one time to sing your song for the first time to your Lady."

Joe Sr.:	"I practiced for days listening to Marvin, watching Marvin, talking like Marvin, walking like Marvin, and grooving like Marvin."
Joe Sr.:	"I had become Marvin Gaye, and for one day each year, I am still Marvin Gaye."
Joe Sr.:	"Now, here's an important historical side note."
Joe Sr.:	"A couple of years ago Clyde Grace, Mary's father, took my song, after I showed it to him, and made it his song too."
Joe Sr.:	"So if this ever comes up in conversation, just smile and act like you know nothing."
Joseph:	"Ok Dad. Just for grins and giggles, will Mr. Grace's account of this story match yours?"
Joe Sr.:	"Son he's a good man, so I'm going to plead the 5th on this one."
Joseph:	"Got it Dad. You picked the song and Mr. Grace helped you with your dance moves."
Joe Sr.:	"How do you know that? I meant who told you that?"
Joseph:	"Let's just say the walls have eyes and ears Dad."
Joseph:	"Plus everyone knows Mr. Grace can cut a rug."
Joseph:	"Not like you Dad. Your moves are next level for sure and absolutely out of this world."

(Joseph can't contain the laugh and Joe Sr. chuckles too reminiscing about the past.)

Joseph:	"I'm pretty sure you only needed his help to dial back the complexity of your moves so us mere mortals could enjoy them too."
Joe Sr.:	"Joseph you are too silly for school."
Joseph:	"Like father like son."

(Joseph's last comment goes totally unnoticed by Joe Sr. who picks up right where he left off.)

Where There's Faith There's Grace

Joe Sr.:	"In my mind I had become Marvin and that made me fearless. I wasn't afraid to show or tell anyone how I felt about your momma."
Joe Sr.:	"So I'm sharing this with you Joseph, with one request, and that is, when it's time, you share your story with your boys too."
Joseph:	"Davidson swear for life Pops."
Joe Sr.:	"Now this is where it gets real."
Joe Sr.:	"Moments before I went to sing my song to woo your mother, your grandfather cornered me and said these words."
Joe Sr.:	"Son, I know what you've been thinking. I can see it on your forehead every time you forget to do something I told you to do today two weeks ago."
Joe Sr.:	"I know how much you love this girl, so go sing her your song today with Davidson pride. Yes, that same song you've been practicing for 33 days, 12 hours, and 13 seconds."
Joe Sr.:	"Just keep the moves to a minimum. You don't want to scare the young lady off."

(Joe Sr. whispers to Joseph.)

Joe Sr.:	"How did he know?"
Joe Sr.:	"Years later, my Dad told me that all Davidsons have a talent for singing and doing Big Things."
Joe Sr.:	"But the greatest Davidson of them all, wrote, sang, and danced to many, many songs."
Joe Sr.:	"His work put all these supposed greats to shame."
Joe Sr.:	"You ever hear of Michael Jackson dancing himself right out of his own clothes?"
Joseph:	"Dad are you saying that we are related to the King of Pop?"
Joe Sr.:	"No, I'm talking about King David son."

Joseph:	"Dad, that's bananas. David the slayer of giants and killer of lions was an entertainer?"
Joe Sr.:	"Yes. I know it can be hard to believe, but it's all true. Check it out. It's in the Word."
Joe Sr.:	"So you can see why this is a big thing for the sons of David?"
Joseph:	"Yes, especially when you say it can be verified in the Word. You know what I mean?"
Joe Sr.:	"Shifting gears for a moment son. Before I get to the big finish and you go full speed past the point of no return, i.e. "I Do.""
Joe Sr.:	"I have to throw you a fast ball up and in a little sweet chin music, to knock you down, and back you away from the plate. So it ain't so easy for you to swing for the fences on your first at-bat."
Joe Sr.:	"So before you say 'I do", you and I are going to see a man about a horse."
Joseph:	"First outer space, then songwriting, jumped over to baseball and now horseracing, Dad how tall does this "tall tale" really get?"
Joe Sr.:	"I was talking about going to the track Joseph. The baseball was just a metaphor."
Joe Sr.:	"But it's all a lead-in to the one universal truth of Husbandry."
Joe Sr.:	"That once you put on those golden handcuffs (rings), you'll never ever, ever, ever, ever be able to just go off and do anything that you like to do without first, asking for, and then receiving permission."
Joseph:	"Permission Dad, isn't that a little extreme too?"
Joe Sr.:	"Yes, but no Joseph."
Joe Sr.:	"Think about this, when was the last time you saw me do anything outside of work alone?"
Joseph:	"Never."

Joe Sr.:	"When was the last time you heard your mother ask me, "Where have you been Joseph?""
Joseph:	"Never, again."
Joe Sr.:	"And that's a good thing son."
Joe Sr.:	"The reason I say permission is because it's hard to see it as anything else, especially when you're a young man and full of yourself."
Joe Sr.:	"My mother used to say to my father "Baby, he's just smelling his britches."
Joseph:	"I hope that was a metaphor too Dad."
Joe Sr.:	"The point of it all Joseph, is that the older I got, my perspective shifted from seeing it as asking for permission, to thanking your mother for the protection she provided me by being concerned."
Joseph:	"I now see the error in my previous thinking. I'm glad I'm learning this now from you Dad and not from the world."
Joe Sr.:	"I'm glad you respect me enough to sit and listen son."
Joe Sr.:	"I really learned to embrace the protection that is created from accountability."
Joe Sr.:	"Seeing my boys go down in flames one-by-one, due to idle time spent with idle minds was the biggest eye opener ever."
Joe Sr.:	"So as I matured, I was able to step back and actually see what the world really had to offer me."
Joe Sr.:	"Which, Joseph is what?"
Joseph:	"NOTHING!!!"
Joe Sr.:	"And because of that fact, I learned to love your mother even more for protecting us both."
Joe Sr.:	"And I didn't think I could love her any more than I already did."
Joe Sr.:	"I thought I had maxed out my love at "I Do.""

Joe Sr.:	"Boy, was I wrong. Love is amazing and it will continue to grow beyond your wildest imagination."
Joe Sr.:	"Especially when the two of you build it together and allow God to direct your steps."
Joe Sr.:	"Each day, if you choose, you can awaken a brand-new person to a brand-new person."
Joseph:	"That's deep Dad. Can you share a little more about what love means to you?"
Joe Sr.:	"Yes I can. Love comes from God, Joseph. Because God is love, so for me love becomes much easier to understand when you understand Him."
Joe Sr.:	"God's love is not this mystical feeling or potion. It begins with your submission to being loved by God as God defines love."
Joe Sr.:	"Accepting the fact that the greatest power in the universe, who knows every cell in your body has an intense desire to want to know you even deeper than that."
Joe Sr.:	"And here's the kicker, he provided us a learner's manual called; His Word."
Joe Sr.:	"Read from it daily and meditate on its meaning. Praying to God for your eyes to see it as God's mouth spoke it, and to hear it as God's messengers wrote it."
Joe Sr.:	"When you do those things, you will be prepared to begin the journey of growing into the role of the head of, and not ruler of your home."
Joseph:	"Great, now I have to check throne off my side of the wedding registry."

(Joe Sr. can only shake his head.)

Joe Sr.:	"Son, real talk. When you equip yourself with this knowledge, you will have established the foundation to love that woman with all you have for as long as you have."

Joe Sr.:	"Make sense?"
Joseph:	"Yes it does Dad. And thanks for sharing Old Wise One."
Joseph:	"Are you sure you're not related to Yoda?"
Joe Sr.:	"Hmmm, much to learn you still have."
Joseph:	"What!!! Improvisation skills too. Nice Padre."
Joseph:	"But back to your explanation of love. If I heard you correctly."
Joseph:	"When I submit myself to God's will and make his ways my ways, I become capable of treating my wife as God treats us all."
Joe Sr.:	"Yes Joseph and Amen. You have touched my soul with those words."
Joe Sr.:	"Kind of like the time you told your mother and I you were moving out and made us promise not to talk you out of it."
Joe Sr.:	"You didn't know it at the time, but we earned Academy Awards that evening and celebrated like it was 1999 once you went to your room."
Joseph:	"Ha, Ha, Ha, Dad, I knew you were hurting inside."

(Joe Sr. was a perfect father's blend of sarcasm and love.)

Joseph:	"Anyway, I have much to learn Dad. But your words give me hope and they increase my desire to learn so much more about what God expects from me as a man and husband."
Joseph:	"These words have allowed me to reflect back in just this brief amount of time to see how you were always teaching me the Lord's principles and preparing me for this conversation, preparing me for this moment."
Joseph:	"I never truly realized the importance and full impact of having a loving and God-fearing father until now."

Joseph:	"You know Dad, there are so many young men out there who are missing all that comes from one of the three most important relationships they need to have growing up."
Joseph:	"Most are literally flying by the seat of their pants and making it up as they go."
Joseph:	"Dad I'm not afraid to admit that I'd be lost without you."
Joseph:	"You have taught me so much by your example."
Joseph:	"I know that if I don't live the life that God requires of me, my marriage has no chance, that I have no chance."
Joseph:	"And everything about me will be a failure if I get to the end of the race alone and without doing right by my family."
Joe Sr.:	"Joseph you are ON IT!!!!"

Joe Sr. without thinking and without hesitation busts a couple of the moves he has become renowned for. He looked at Joseph, pounded his heart, pointed to Heaven, closed his eyes, and shared a moment unafraid to let the tears of joy fall down his face. Joe Sr. composes himself and returns to the conversation.

Joe Sr.:	"Baby boy, we're finally here at the end of today's story, which is sharing my song."
Joe Sr.:	"I have kept this cassette tape and boom box for 40 years, now I want you to sit down over there and study and learn the ways of the Davidson men."
Joseph:	"Dad I know this is going to be epic because everything you do is over the top."
Joseph:	"So hold on so I can set up my cell phone."
Joe Sr.:	"Take your time. I want you to have this so you can properly prepare to show that Ms. Grace just how much she means to you."
Joe Sr.:	"Make your song something she'll never forget."
Joe Sr.:	"Just make it last forever and everrrrr."

(In his best Keith Sweat voice.)

Joe Sr.:   "Joseph this is my song, there are many like it, but this one is mine."

Joe Sr.:   "I want you to hear the words and to watch the moves because they are both part of the story that led to you."

(Joe Sr. cues his music and takes his mark in the middle of the shop.)

(Joseph notices that his father is standing on the same piece of blue painters tape he saw on the floor early that morning.)

Joe Sr.:   "Push play my man."

Joseph presses play and the music to Marvin Gaye's "I Want You" flows through the speakers like it was 1976 and in that moment, he witnessed his father transform. He was Marvin Gaye and Joseph knew he was recording something incredible. He was watching his past, present, and future merge into this moment.

(The song faded out softly and Marvin Gaye and Joe Sr. did bid each other adieu once again.)

The two men needed only to stand and look at each other. Knowing if you have seen the father, you have seen the son and vice versa.

Joe Sr.:   "I love you always son."

Joseph: "I love you always Dad."

Joe Sr. and Joseph walk out the shop and close the door behind them.

(Lights off.)

(Curtains.)

Stacy Lamar King

Act One

Scene Three

With This Ring

It is Sunday evening in Hampton Park. It is a park known for its long and winding trails, green grasses, and majestic trees. The park is festive and teeming with families, couples, horse and carriages, street musicians, vendors in all shapes and sizes, cops, and also cons.

Flowing with the rhythm of Charleston, Joseph and Mary find themselves alone in their favorite place in the world, their nook, a park within a park.

Like moments in love, the events of this evening, will mark the beginning of their journey together.

Mary:	"Joseph I just love this park."
Mary:	"Whenever we're here, I'm happy."
Joseph:	"You too. I thought it was just me this whole time."

(It was deja vu all over again.)

Mary:	"Baby I know you invited me here to tell me something special, but before you do."

(Mary pauses for effect.)

Mary:	"I need you to sit down and close your eyes."
Mary:	"I want you to listen to the words I'm about to write, right here on your heart."

Mary traced her finger around Joseph's heart. When she finished, she walked him towards the park bench and seated him right there. There were butterflies present everywhere. Mary took a moment to compose herself.

(From a small speaker next to the bench came the voice of Mary's favorite DJ.)

DJ Soul:	"Hey Mary, we're riding with you and Joseph tonight."
DJ Soul:	"Here's the instrumentals from your girl Goapele's "Closer to My Dreams."
DJ Soul:	"Remember the world is yours."

With that, Mary starts a new tradition for the women in her family. A song about her man. Her dream.

Joseph stood and watched in amazement at the way Mary moved. She was Goapele just like his father had become Marvin. It was life imitating life. And when Mary finished her song, Joseph hugged her tightly, extending the joy of this moment.

Mary's courage had eased Joseph's butterflies too and he was now poised to share his song with his lady. Looking confidently towards the heavens and filled with the Spirit. Joseph seized the moment, like a Davidson man.

Joseph:	"Mary its happening isn't it's?"
Joseph:	"This is our moment."
Joseph:	"The one we dreamed about."
Joseph:	"It's happening right now baby."
Joseph:	"It's not a dream."
Joseph:	"You're so beautiful tonight it's hard to look at you."
Joseph:	"Hard to believe you're my lady."
Joseph:	"I know I may sound crazy, but that's how I'm feeling right now."
Joseph:	"Mary, this is my song about you girl."
Joseph:	"I call it Mary's Grace."
Joseph:	"Please take a seat Baby."

Mary shakes her head cutely, choosing to stand because she didn't think she could stay seated. A quartet appeared out of the night shadows and Mary was blown away.

The band struck the first note of Musiq Soulchild's "So Beautiful" and Joseph became Musiq Soulchild. Singing this song, his song, from the heart, and claiming his lady before the Heavens.

Joseph brought it home and members of both families came in from the shadows. They watched quietly as Joseph took a knee and began to propose to their very own little Ms. Mary Grace.

Joseph: "Mary I want you to place your hand right here."

(She flashed that million-dollar smile at Joseph.)

Joseph: "Can you feel my heart beating for you?"

(Mary nods yes as their hearts raced.)

Joseph: "Please keep your hand there because your touch is the only thing that calms my heart."

Joseph: "From this day forward, this is our symbol and our promise to one another."

Joseph: "The thing that brings us back to this moment when life makes us forget where we came from."

Joseph: "Your heart is the special place where I find my joy."

Joseph: "It's you and me baby. One heartbeat for a life time."

Mary had imagined this moment her whole life and yet her imagination had never equaled what she was feeling and experiencing right now.

(Joseph took a knee.)

Joseph: "Ms. Mary Grace, woman of my dreams, whom I will cherish all the days of my life."

Joseph: "Will you marry me?"

Mary prayed and remained as composed as she could even though she felt like running and jumping into Joseph's arms.

Mary: "YESSSSSSSSSS!!!! A thousand times yes Joseph."

Joseph took Mary's trembling hand within his own, both shaking then calming together, and placed the ring on Mary's finger.

Mary: "Joseph, I will never forget this moment for as long as my soul shall exist."

Joseph: "I know."

Camera flashes light the night like candles. It was magical and beautiful. A lasting memory for the young and the old alike.

(The parties depart the park.)

(Curtains.)

Act Two

Scene One

The Fork in the Road

It is 30 minutes before sunset in Hampton Park. The park is both quiet and bustling. Mary is seated on her bench reminiscing about her engagement to Joseph and peacefully planning the rest of their lives together.

Dreams do come true and Mary pinches herself to make sure. With a Daisy in her hand, she recalls the words to Joseph's song as she waits for the sunset, her favorite moment of the day.

Mary: "He loves me now. He'll love me later."

Mary: "This love's good. That loves greater."

(Daisy petals fall loudly to the ground.)

Mary: "I love this man. I love the God that made him."

Mary stops picking the petals after looking down at her feet and noticing what she has done to the once beautiful daisy.

(A stranger appears mysteriously as if out of thin air.)

Gabe: "Good evening my Lady."

(Mary sits unaware of the stranger's words as thoughts of Joseph run non-stop through her mind.)

(Gabe shrewdly clears his throat to gain Mary's attention.)

Gabe: "Eh hmm."

Gabe: "Oh my, what a beautiful day the Lord has made."

Gabe: "Like you, I too, am waiting to see the sunset."

Mary is astonished by the stranger's sudden appearance and boldness. She searches her memory trying to recall the moment she first noticed him.

Gabe: "Do you mind if I sit here to share this sunset?"

(Mary nods nonchalantly.)

Gabe: "You know, I have stared at sunsets millions of times from afar but I must admit that nothing truly compares to this view right here."

(Mary vaguely listens to the utterings of the stranger, unsure of the destination of this conversation and still pondering how this bizarre looking man might know her.)

Gabe: "Do you mind if I call you Mary?"

(Mary suddenly looks among the crowd for her friends and the man holding the hidden camera.)

Mary: "OK, do we know each other?"

Gabe: "Mary you don't know me, but I have known you forever."

Gabe: "But, more important than that, I have come to deliver the greatest news you're ever going to hear."

Mary becomes more skeptical as the vibe she's getting from this man makes the hidden camera bit now seem out of the question. So, she impatiently awaits the inevitable sales pitch.

Gabe: "Mary, of all the women in the world my Lord has found great favor in you."

Gabe: "He wants you to know that the example you have set makes you worthy."

(Mary can feel herself becoming frustrated.)

Mary: "What????"

Mary:	"Mister, I can only assume that you have come from clear across the pond, because no one in Charleston talks like that, and NO ONE calls their boss, their Lord."

(Gabe is unfamiliar with Mary's pond reference.)

Gabe:	"Mary my Lord walks with you every day and has chosen you to be a part of the greatest love story ever written."

(Mary listens half-heartedly.)

Mary:	"Gabe if that is your real name do you not see this ice on my finger."
Mary:	"A blind man could see that I am spoken for."

(Gabe literally scans Mary's hand for ice.)

Gabe:	"No disrespect intended Mary. Since I don't see the presence of ice, I can only assume that you are referring to that ring on your finger."

(Mary sits speechless.)

Gabe:	"Hmmm. This is not going well is it?"

(Crickets.)

Gabe:	"Let me try this again, if I may."

(Mary, against her better judgment begrudgingly nods yes.)

Gabe:	"Mary, I didn't properly introduce myself and that was indeed very rude of me."

(Gabe slowly recognizes that a sudden appearance out of thin air doesn't have quite the impact it had 6000 years ago.)

Gabe:	"I assure you that my name is Gabe."
Gabe:	"And, you are correct in assuming I am not from Charleston."

Gabe: "I hail from an exquisite place far from here."

Gabe: "It's beyond Paradise and I love my job."

Gabe: "The tasks that I am most honored to fulfill are the delivery of important messages from my Lord."

Gabe: "The kind that absolutely, positively, must make it there overnight."

(Gabe chuckles and snaps his fingers to emphasize this point.)

(Mary sits without blinking.)

Gabe: "Messages much like the one I am delivering to you right now."

Mary can't tell if he's a messenger or conman. Either way she's ready for this conversation to come to an end. Sensing the change in Mary's disposition, Gabe knows he must now improvise.

Gabe: "Mary I know you came to the park this evening to watch the sunset like you have many times before and I can see the love you have for this Joseph fella in everything you've thought, said, and done this evening."

(Gabe's words strike a chord and bring a mixture of calmness, curiosity, and relaxation to Mary.)

Gabe: "Mary, I'm glad to see that you are a little more at ease."

Mary tries to look intently at Gabe, yet is unable to hold the gaze. He looks so unique, unlike anyone she has ever seen.

Gabe: "This message was written long ago and has been passed down for many years."

Gabe: "Tonight, I am delivering it to its intended recipient and it will culminate in the fulfillment of a promise my Lord made to the world a long time ago."

(Gabe noticed that the weight of his words were beginning to weigh heavily upon Mary's heart.)

Gabe:	"Mary please don't be afraid. My Lord has examined your spirit and found you alone and ready for this work."
Gabe:	"You see Mary, you are going to become a mother very soon and you will give birth to a beautiful son. A son you will name Jesus, which means God saves and he will be called the Son of the Most-High."
Mary:	"When the time is right my Lord will place your son upon the throne. The throne that his forefather David sat upon and he will reign as King and His Kingdom and His people will live forever."
Mary:	"Hold Up…. Wait a Minute…."
Mary:	"Before I call you crazy let me make sure I heard you correctly."
Mary:	"If my memory serves me right, you've said Joseph whom I love dearly, who, like me is relatively broke and unknown right here in our own town, will become a King which we here in the United States of America call a President, and I, his First Lady."
Mary:	"And then you said Joseph and I are going to have a baby boy and that's cool but we're going to name him Jesus, which is not a very popular name in these parts. Might I add, that our baby boy is going to become an even greater President than his father."
Mary:	"What!!!"
Mary:	"Did I miss anything?"

(Gabe was speechless and he paused to digest all that he had heard so that he might form a sensible reply.)

Mary:	"Gabe, we have to take a selfie of this moment."
Mary:	"I have to post this on my Facebook page right now, because none of my girlfriends will ever believe this story without visual proof."

(Gabe notes this dramatic detour from the intent of the messages, and says with EXTREME emphasis.)

Gabe: "Mary in the name of all that is Holy and for your spiritual and physical health, you must not attempt to take my picture with that thing."

To date no one had ever tried this, so there was no Heavenly protocol, and Gabe wasn't altogether sure what would happen, but he did know that it wouldn't bode well for Mary.

Gabe: "Nor Mary, must you make a single mention of this conversation or of me to anyone, to include those you love dearly, and especially to those you know in your Book of Faces."

(Mary notes his utter disdain for Facebook and can only deduce that he must have been cyber bullied in his past.)

Gabe: "Now Mary, please pay close attention. The words I'm about to share with you are meant only for you."

Gabe: "These words will come to define everything about you."

Gabe: "They will take your breath away and raise your spirit to the Heavens.

Gabe: "And at other times they will put you on your knees."

Gabe: "But the Lord will be with you through it all."

Gabe: "You will soon become a living witness to the Lord's awesome power and you will experience it like no other woman."

Gabe: "Mary, the decision that you are already making in your heart will set in motion a series of events that were foretold by the ancient of days before there were days."

Gabe: "The events I have spoke of will ripple throughout the universe and the Heavens forever."

Gabe: "So please, please, please, listen very, very, carefully to the remainder of what I have to say to you."

Gabe:	"The Lord's Holy Spirit will soon come upon you and the power of the Most-High will cover you."
Gabe:	"You will know exactly when it happens, and because of this, you will conceive a Holy Child, unique in every way, that there will be no other like him or after him, and he will be called by many the Son of the Most-High."

(Mary sits stoically as her heart and mind race 100 miles an hour.)

Gabe:	"I know you have many questions you want to ask me. They will be answered in due time, this I assure you because this is Lord's promise to you."
Gabe:	"But, before I bid you adieu, here's something that you will enjoy reading, something that will help open your mind to the total context of this message."
Gabe:	"I want you to open the oldest of your ancient apps, one that I know about; I believe you and your kind call it Google."
Gabe:	"Search for the story of the Miracle Baby of Columbia."
Gabe:	"When you read it, it will make what was once hazy crystal clear."

(Gabe stood, looked down at Mary, and flashed a smile that was brighter than a thousand moons.)

Mary Googled the story of the Miracle Baby of Columbia and when it popped up her soul was instantly filled with the Holy Spirit. She recognized the image of her great-great-cousin Liz Beth, who had no children, yet was now in her old age pregnant with child.

Mary opened her mouth to empty words. She fell to her knees and then collected herself and spoke to the Lord from her heart.

Mary:	"Dear Lord I will pray day and night that you continue to find favor in me, that your will be accomplished through me, so that no matter how hard things get, or how hard it becomes for my mind to comprehend, I will still believe."
Mary:	"Lord, I surrender my life to you right now. My life is your life and your will is my will."

When Mary finished her prayer, she looked up, her eyes blinking repeatedly and noticed that Gabe was gone. He had vanished in the same way that he had appeared, into thin air.

Mary:	"I have been visited by an Angel."

Mary knelt down and picked up the Daisy petals she had thrown to the ground, placing them in her purse as a reminder to remember God's beauty in all things.

(Mary exits the park.)

(Curtains.)

Act Two

Scene Two

When Doves Try

A month had passed since Mary's visitation from Gabe. She did not sleep at all the previous night. From the moment she read the story of her great-cousin, the one she called Auntie Liz Beth, Mary knew she had to get to her as soon as humanly possible. Gabe had given her a clue that she had to investigate.

Mary packed hastily that morning and loaded up a small bag. Her trusty laptop and a small suitcase, leaving a small post-It note for her mother on the refrigerator. She drove with passive aggression, a strange combination for such a young driver. Stopping once along the way for Starbucks and a Snickers, the breakfast of students.

As Mary drove, she thought about how social media had taken the story of her cousin Liz Beth to the four corners of the world. The story had become so big that Liz Beth had literally become a prisoner in her own home just to avoid the circus.

Not fully knowing what to expect, Mary believed that meeting with Liz Beth would give her a deeper understanding of God's plan and her role within it.

(Mary arrived at Liz Beth's home, and entered with a glow about her, and amazement in her eyes.)

Mary:	"Auntie I had to leave Charleston as soon as I could."
Mary:	"My face literally hit the ground when a search revealed that you were glowing and pregnant."
Mary:	"I knew at that very moment, that you would be the only person in the whole universe who could listen and understand what has happened to me."
Mary:	"Because I'm still in shock."
Mary:	"I mean, I know I have faith, but it is the faith that was instilled in me by my parent's."

Mary:	"So how can I, knowing so little, carry the living Son of God within me?"
Mary:	"Yesterday my life was Facebook, school, clothes, Joseph, and sometimes music."
Mary:	"Now I, Mary Grace, Most Likely to Never Leave Charleston 2014, am supposed to become the mother of the Son of God."
Mary:	"Liz Beth, we're talking about the Almighty God here. The Most-High."
Mary:	"Here's me, here's the Lord, me, the Lord, me, the Lord."

(Mary uses the distance from her hand to the ground to demonstrate her limitations as compared to the unlimited power of the Lord.)

Mary:	"And, what do I say to Joseph?"

(Mary demonstrates the beginning of her conversation about the Holy Child with Joseph using the only medium she knows, humor.)

Mary:	"Knock, Knock"
Joseph:	"Who's There?"
Mary:	"Pregnant."
Joseph:	"Says Who?"
Mary:	"The Lord."
Joseph:	"The Lord?"
Mary:	"YES, THE LORD!"
Mary:	"Auntie can't you see that I'm freaking out here?"
Liz Beth:	"Calm down precious."
Liz Beth:	"From the moment you walked through our doors, I could feel my son doing cart wheels."
Liz Beth:	"And I knew right then that you were carrying the Messiah inside you."
Liz Beth:	"I am so honored to have you here."
Liz Beth:	"The Holy Spirit walks with you."

Liz Beth:	"I know you believe you're coming here to strengthen your faith. I think you were sent here to strengthen mine as well."
Liz Beth:	"Sit down so I can tell you our story."

(Liz Beth escorted Mary to the sofa in the living room. She then departed to the kitchen and returned with two glasses of water with lemon slices.)

Liz Beth:	"Your Uncle Zach received a message like you did from an Angel of the Lord."
Liz Beth:	"It happened about six months ago, early on a Saturday morning as he prepared to lead morning worship across the 12 campuses."
Liz Beth:	"Now you know your uncle has served the church faithfully for forty years and leading service across the campuses on the Sabbath was something he had waited so patiently for."
Liz Beth:	"For him it was a once in a life-time opportunity, and as the day unfolded, he just happened to be in the right place at the right time, doing the right thing for all the right reasons."
Mary:	"Providence."
Liz Beth:	"Did you say providence? Where did you learn that word Mary?"
Mary:	"Yes I did. It's a long story. I'll tell you one day."

(They chuckle in unison.)

Liz Beth:	"But baby Zach's story is both one of wonder and caution."
Liz Beth:	"The outcome of his conversation with the Angel of the Lord is a lesson for us all."
Liz Beth:	"A reminder that the things that seem impossible in our minds are not so for the Lord."
Liz Beth:	"During Zach's conversation with the Angel he questioned the Lord's ability to perform the miracle that would give us a son and he has not spoken a word since."

Mary:	"Really?"
Liz Beth:	"Really."
Liz Beth:	"Mary, your faith is going to be tried and tested throughout your life. Sometimes caused by yourself."
Liz Beth:	"And in my heart, I believe the Lord weeps each time one of his children is tripped up by a lack of trust in the promises found within His Word."
Liz Beth:	"So we must either believe the Lord is who He said He is, or we do not, by choosing to put our human limitations on His infinite power."
Liz Beth:	"Interesting fact, even though Zach can't speak right now, his writing is remarkable, and who knew he could learn and teach me sign language in such short order at our age."
Liz Beth:	"He has provided some amazing scriptural notes for me to share with you today."
Liz Beth:	"I believe these notes will confirm what you already know to be true."
Mary:	"What's that Auntie Liz Beth?"
Liz Beth:	"That nothing is impossible for the Lord."
Liz Beth:	"Everything that was, is, and will be, is a part of the Lord's master plan to restore our relationship with Him."
Liz Beth:	"You, Mary Grace, are a key part of His plan."
Liz Beth:	"Before we start, let's bow our heads in prayer to ask for the Lord's blessing."

Liz Beth and Mary pray a simple prayer to the Lord, asking that his Words shine like a light in the darkness of their minds and burn like a fire in the depths of their souls.

Liz Beth:	"Mary, let's go over the steps the Lord has taken to establish His plan for our salvation."

Liz Beth:	"Step #1, The Lord established a people of his own – Out of a sea of unbelievers the Lord found one faithful man in the Earth, and through him He established a covenant and called his descendants Hebrews and they became His chosen people."
Liz Beth:	"Step #2, over time the Lord entrusted His people with knowledge of the Holy Oracles – Prophesies. Showing the Heavenly and Earthly path of His Son to His people."
Liz Beth:	"Step #3, The Lord established the blood line from which the Savior of the world, your Son would come from – The Chosen Line of King David who was a descendent of Abraham."
Liz Beth:	"Step #4, The Lord identified His people as the nation that all Heavenly blessings would flow through. The 12 tribes of Israel."
Mary:	"Whoa. It's so clear. So simple. His lineage and his identity are undeniable."
Liz Beth:	"Absolutely Mary."

(Liz Beth moves on to the personal stages of the Lord's plan brought to life.)

Liz Beth:	"Whew, I made it through the first part. Now let's look at how the Lord has used the Hebrew patriarchs and matriarchs to fulfill his plan."
Liz Beth:	"It all starts with Abraham (the chosen one), who was selected to be the father of many nations."
Liz Beth:	"The prophets detail how and why Abraham migrated into the land the Lord promised him."
Liz Beth:	"It is essential that you gain a deeper understanding of these prophesies."
Liz Beth:	"The Lord has always prepared his people for the future by the evidence of events from the past."

Liz Beth:	"The miracle birth of Isaac to Abraham and his wife Sarah is just one of many that we can all follow directly to you."
Liz Beth:	"Right upon the heel of Isaac came the Holy birth of Jacob."
Liz Beth:	"The major point is that the Lord never shows you something that hasn't been explained beforehand. He builds every layer of His Word, precept upon precept."
Liz Beth:	"Do you see and understand this key point Mary?"
Mary:	"I most certainly do Auntie and this has cleared my mind immensely."
Mary:	"That's great news. I wasn't sure I could do this as well as Zach, and I was afraid that I might return you to Charleston more confused than you arrived here."
Mary:	"Auntie, the Lord is with you. You are doing so well and my spirit is lifted."

(With that Liz Beth took the message for Mary a little deeper.)

Liz Beth:	"Mary the Lord knows you're young and He doesn't require perfection."
Liz Beth:	"In every step of His plan He has used broken vessels to bake beautiful bread."
Liz Beth:	"They have all faltered and yet through their faith and His grace, they persevered."
Liz Beth:	"Let's look again at Abraham and Sarah."
Liz Beth:	"Abraham feared the Pharaoh more than he trusted the Lord's protection and because of that Sarah ended up inside the Pharaoh's quarters."
Liz Beth:	"And Sarah, well she didn't trust the Lord's timeline and gave her slave girl to Abraham and she became the mother of his first-born Son."

Liz Beth:	"Key point neither of these events disrupted the Lord's plan. It flows like a river."
Liz Beth:	"Do you see how His power covers a multitude of sins specifically the loss of faith?"
Mary:	"Yes, it's as clear as the sky is blue."
Liz Beth:	"Abraham and Sarah were blessed with the miracle of birth and a son named Isaac."
Liz Beth:	"Now Isaac married Rebecca and they had twins named Esau and Jacob."
Liz Beth:	"The Lord told Rebecca that the first child would grow to serve the second."
Mary:	"If I remember correctly, Rebecca favored Jacob and Isaac favored Esau because he was a great hunter."
Liz Beth:	"I am very impressed at your ability to see below the surface of things."
Liz Beth:	"You can see how that might become a problem?"
Mary:	"Yes, it still happens, in families right now."
Mary:	"You can thank my parents for what I know."
Liz Beth:	"Baby, they may have taught you how to ride the bike, but you little lady, are riding the bike on your own right now."
Liz Beth:	"That brings me to the last couple in this string of miracle births."
Liz Beth:	"Jacob, the son of Isaac, struggled in just about every way a man could, falling short in so many ways."
Liz Beth:	"Towards the end of his life, his barren wife, Rachel, was blessed with a beautiful son named Joseph who would go on to become one of the Godliest men to walk the Earth."
Liz Beth:	"Long story short, Rachel wasn't content with one miracle. She prayed for another and she would die during the child birth of her second son Benjamin."

Mary:	Auntie, they were all broken together, falling constantly, crawling when they couldn't walk, yet joined for life through it all, because of their faith and the grace of God.
Mary:	"Auntie, each of these marriages offers life lessons that all couples can use to strengthen their walk with the Lord."
Mary:	"It is the Lord's union with the husband and wife that resonates most with me."
Mary:	"I can see how the triangle loses its strength when either the leg of the husband or the wife breaks or bows."

(Zach walks in and signs to Liz Beth.)

Zach:	"Seeing the two of you working together is like glimpsing into Heaven."
Zach:	"You bring tears of joy to my face."

(Liz Beth repeats Zach's message to Mary.)

(Liz Beth and Mary thank Zach for his kind words and pick up the conversation from where it had paused.)

Mary:	"Auntie, it seems that I have been surrounded by people like my parents, you, and Uncle Zach my entire life."
Liz Beth:	"Mary, life can be as complex or as simple as we make it, but your knowledge of God begins at home, and both you and Joseph, come from strong God-fearing parents who love you both with their whole heart."
Liz Beth:	"And now you look like a woman who knows the answers to the questions she arrived here with."
Mary:	"Auntie, I feel a peace, like I have never felt before."
Liz Beth:	"Blessed are you Mary, for now, and forever."
Liz Beth:	"Just remember, yours is not to wonder why, but instead, to believe through faith, in what the Lord has revealed to you."
Liz Beth:	"You are part of His Word."

Liz Beth:	"I know it was the questions that drove you here, but you were only confirming what you already knew in your spirit."
Liz Beth:	"Thank you for blessing me with your presence today."
Liz Beth:	"Now I must go see how Zach is doing. He gets so cranky when he's hungry."

(They both laugh lightly.)

Liz Beth:	"You're welcome to join us for lunch if you like."
Mary:	"Thanks for the offer Auntie, but, right now, I am so filled with the spirit, I don't need anything else."
Liz Beth:	"I can see that baby girl. The kitchen is always open for you, so let me know when you're ready to eat, because we have got to get some meat on those bones girl."
Liz Beth:	"Zach has prepared the guest room for you upstairs. Please stay as long as you need."
Liz Beth:	"Meditate on what we have discussed, and when the time is right, go home to him."

(Lights fade as Liz Beth and Mary stand to embrace.)

(Curtains.)

Stacy Lamar King

Act Two

Scene Three

The Reasons Why

The frost of winter has given way to the beauty of spring, that special time of the year when the quaintness of the city is encased in comfort.

Mary is on her way home from Columbia with a deeper understanding of the Good News. The sudden trip to Columbia, her sometimes sporadic and cryptic communications, and the length of her stay, has caused Joseph to question everything about them and himself.

Joseph has loved the Lord and Mary with all his heart, all his life, but has felt all alone in Charleston without her.

He had withdrawn from the world, and built walls so high, that no one could see inside them.

It is late in the evening, after a long day's work, and Joseph is alone in the shop trying to keep his mind occupied with work.

He sits then paces, talking inside his head, then aloud, trying to relax his mind. But he can't stop wrestling with his thoughts, and works himself into a frenzy.

Joseph:	"Mary, me, the Lord and the Messiah. How?"
Joseph:	"I don't understand."
Joseph:	"I was doing good. As good as I could be."
Joseph:	"I am nobody."
Joseph:	"Lord, forgive me because I do not see a way out of this."
Joseph:	"How can I fulfill your plan?"
Joseph:	"I don't know what to do."

Joseph: "I can't believe this is happening."

Joseph: "I woke up this morning so in love and now I feel so confused."

Joseph picked up a glass and shattered it on the closest wall, but that wasn't enough. So he proceeded to kick every paint bucket he could find, letting out a scream that made the Angels weep. His heart had been broken into a million small sharp pieces. He felt he had disappointed the Most-High.

(Joseph fell to his knees, sweating profusely, and looked up towards the Heavens and cried out.)

Joseph: 'Whyyyyyy!!!!!!!!!"

(Beating his fists on the floor.)

Joseph: "Lord, I have read every word you have uttered to your Prophets, and I have looked towards them for the example of how a God-fearing man should live."

Joseph: "But I can't find anyone who has faced what I am facing right now."

Joseph: "And I don't know what to do."

Joseph: "If I believe what my heart believes, then I am afraid, because I don't see how any of this is possible."

(A thought pops into Joseph's mind "Return to the Word.")

Joseph: "I'm a simple man and I know the answer has to be in the Word."

Joseph: "Especially when I need help understanding the impossible."

Joseph: "But where do I start?"

Joseph: "Lord please give me a sign tonight."

Joseph: "That I am to assume that the definition of virgin in this instance goes beyond the fleshly thoughts of man."

Joseph:	"Perhaps meaning pure in her spirit and approved for a magnificent first work in your name oh Lord."
Joseph:	"I pray Lord that my thoughts aren't far from your meaning."
Joseph:	"To David, you promised to bring forth a King through his seed, his sons, and establish his kingdom."
Joseph:	"I am in that line of kings and sons."

(Joseph is visibly shaken by what this may mean to himself, Mary, and the world.)

Joseph:	"This is a lot to take in and my head is about to explode."
Joseph:	"No one is going to believe this. I can't even believe this."
Joseph:	"I'm a common painter. There is nothing special about me. I'm no Isiah."
Joseph:	"The only way I can see my way out of this situation is to stop this wedding right now. Shut it down."
Joseph:	"But those words feel like poison in my mouth."
Joseph:	"It is so late, and I am tired and torn."
Joseph:	"I can't think about this another minute, I'm giving it to you Lord. That's all I can do."
Joseph:	"I pray that you send me a sign tonight. Something to still my heart. Something to hang my hat on."

And with that Joseph laid down on that old scruffy sofa in the back of the shop. The one that has put everyone who has laid upon it in traction. He chose that pain over this pain.

He tossed and turned, wrestling within his mind, until an Angel of the Lord appeared to him in his dreams.

Angel: "Oh Joseph, son of David, do not fear taking Mary as your wife, for the child she carries is by the Holy Spirit."

Angel: "Mary will give birth to a son, and yes you Joseph are his father. You are to name him Jesus because, he will save his people from their sins."

Angel: "These words were written just for you and they shed light on the Glory and the Grace of the Host of Heavens, fulfilling the Words spoken by the Lord through his Prophets."

Angel: "And look! A Virgin named Mary will become pregnant and will give birth to a son who the people will call Immanuel."

Angel: "I delivered this same message to Isiah. Just as I am delivering it to you tonight."

Angel: "Sleep in peace Joseph, your questions have been answered, you are approved."

(With that the Angel departed from Joseph's dream and he did rest.)

(Curtains.)

Act Three

Scene One

I Do

It's early Saturday morning on the day the Lord has made for Joseph and Mary to become one. They had made it to the church on time.

Joseph stood with legs trembling at the alter as Mr. Grace walked his beautiful bride down the aisle.

Mary looked positively stunning.

(The Minister who had known them since they were children commenced the ceremony.)

Minister:	"Joseph and Mary, your marriage today is the public and legal joining of souls that have already been united in your hearts."
Minister:	"Marriage will provide you with a unique place to share your lives together."
Minister:	"Standing together, like you are now, prepared to face life and the world, together."
Minister:	"Marriage is going to expand you as a man and a woman, define you as a couple, and deepen your love for one another."
Minister:	"To be successful, you're going to need strength, courage, patience, and a really good sense of humor."

(Laughter flutters through the church.)

Minister:	"So let your marriage be a time of waking each morning and falling in love all over again."

(The Minister pauses and passes the microphone to Joseph.)

Mary and Joseph faced their friends and sang their song to their world. They thought long and hard about this song and had settled on Anita Baker's "Sweet Love."

(They ended the duet and their guests erupted into applause.)

(Joseph turned to speak to Mary.)

Joseph:	"Today I have found favor with the Lord."
Joseph:	"He has blessed me with the love of my life, and for this my heart is exceedingly glad."
Joseph:	"The Lord has blessed me with a Proverbs 31 woman; a wife of noble character whose worth is far above rubies.
Joseph:	"Mary, I pray that He molds me to be the husband of your dreams but more importantly, a husband with whom He is well pleased."
Joseph:	"Mary, I will be your spiritual cover. I will lead you as the Lord leads me."
Joseph:	"I will love you just as the Lord loves the Church."
Joseph:	"And I will never leave you or forsake you."

(Joseph handed the microphone to Mary. His eyes could not leave hers.)

Mary:	"Today I have found favor with the Lord."
Mary:	"He has blessed me with the love of my life, and for this my heart is exceedingly glad."
Mary:	"Joseph I pray that he molds me to be the wife of your dreams but more importantly a wife with whom He is well pleased."
Mary:	"I will cover you in prayer. I will honor you as the head of our home. I will support you in good times and in bad."
Mary:	"But please do not ever ask me to leave you or turn away from following you."

Mary:	"For wherever you go, I will go, and wherever you pitch your tent, I will pitch mine."
Mary:	"Your people will be my people and your God my God."

(They smile together with their eyes.)

(Mary returns the microphone to the Minister.)

Minister:	"Joseph and Mary, may I remind you that marriage is a precious gift, a lifelong commitment, and a challenge to love one another more completely each and every day."
Minister:	"It is the Lord's work."
Minister:	"Please join hands and look into each other's eyes."
Minister:	"Joseph Davidson, with this understanding do you take Mary Grace to be your wedded wife, to live together in marriage?"
Minister:	"Do you promise to love her, honor and keep her, for better or for worse, for richer or for poorer, in sickness and in health."
Minister:	"Forsaking all others, and to be faithful only to her, for as long as you both shall live?"
Joseph:	"I DO!"
Minister:	"Mary Grace, with this understanding, do you take Joseph Davidson to be your wedded husband, to live together in marriage."
Minister:	"Do you promise to love him, comfort him, honor and keep him, for better or for worse, for richer or for poorer, in sickness and in health."
Minister:	"Forsaking all others, and to be faithful only to him, so long as you both may live?"
Mary:	"Yes I DO!"
Minister:	"May I have the rings please."

(The cute little ring bearers come forward with the rings on a pillow.)

Minister: "Joseph, as you place this ring on Mary's finger, repeat these words after me."

Minister: "This ring, a gift for you, symbolizes my desire, that you be my wife, from this day forward, as this ring has no end, neither shall my love for you."

Minister: "Mary, as you place this ring on Joseph's finger, repeat these words after me."

Minister: "This ring, a gift for you, symbolizes my desire, that you be my husband, from this day forward, as this ring has no end, neither shall my love for you."

Minister: "Joseph Davidson and Mary Grace, I now pronounce you man and wife, you may now kiss the bride."

(They were kissing at "Joseph.")

(Liz Beth quietly walks forward with Zach holding their son Jon.)

(Liz Beth received the microphone from the Minister.)

The Lights fade, and a spotlight settles on Liz Beth, as she softly delivers Sade's "No Ordinary Love" to a new generation of soon to be Sade fans. The song ends and the photographer stages them all for the group wedding shot.

After the group photos were finished, the photographer positioned Joseph and Mary for the one photo that would capture their love and be shared by their children and their children's children forever.

(The Camera Flashes.)

(Curtains.)

Available Wherever Books Are Sold

www.ingramcontent.com/pod-product-compliance
Lightning Source LLC
Chambersburg PA
CBHW061342040426
42444CB00011B/3052